# Catching the Spirit

## Songs of Light and Shadow

**Maureen McCarthy**

ST. BEDE'S PUBLICATIONS
Petersham, Massachusetts

Illustrations by the author

LIBRARY OF CONGRESS CATALOGING-IN-PUBLICATION DATA

McCarthy, Maureen.
   Catching the spirit : songs of light and shadow /
Maureen McCarthy.
      p.   cm.
      Poems.
      ISBN 1-879007-12-6
      I. Title.
PS3563.C337336C37    1994
811'.54--dc20
                                              94-12991
                                              CIP



Published by:  St. Bede's Publications
               P.O. Box 545, North Main St.
               Petersham, MA 01366-0545

# Contents

This book is dedicated lovingly to
Paul,
Jennifer and John,
and their contemporaries
in the hope that they will
continue to seek the spirit,
hold it high, and so be
"a light for all generations."

# *Introduction*

In our search for the Spirit, most of us experience some moments of extraordinary illumination. More frequently, however, we encounter shadows, fog, darkness and discouragement. These poems are about the searching and the discoveries; the seeking, losing, and finding again; about courage, tragedies and pain. They are ultimately about catching and keeping the "Spirit that dwells within."

For many years, keeping a daily journal has provided me with a means of recording insights and reflections. Rereading them often provides a balance between the periods of light and shadow that accompany the daily journey to the inner self. These personal journals are the source of *Catching the Spirit*.

The progress from journal page to publication has been an exciting one. It began with my giving a poem or two to friends in need of encouragement. As requests increased and I discovered how much the poems were appreciated, I collected a small group to give as Christmas gifts each year. This method provided a meaningful way of gathering the poems., Those groups make up the chapters in this book.

Originally, each collection was dedicated to someone who had been a significant inspiration that year. For example, *Songs of Joy* includes memories of a final summer spent with my father-in-law, Eugene McCarthy, Sr.

My mother, Florence Fitzgibbons Goggin, was the natural choice for *Songs for the Journey* as she continues to be a source of light to us all as she enters her 97th year.

A group of longer poetic sequences concentrating on loving commitments comprises *Songs of the Goldfinch*. It considers vows of obedience, chastity and poverty, and the vocation of the married life.

Finally, *Singing in the Silence* celebrates the discovery of a quiet heart and sings especially for my son, Joseph, who died in 1984 at the age of 25.

Recently, a very close friend, Charles Rich, asked to see the entire collection. I complied with his request and in so doing began another kind of journey. At Charles' insistence, I summarized the poetry and submitted it for publication. I was overwhelmed when it was accepted by St. Bede's.

It is now my hope that as you wander through these pages, muse over the designs and reflect on the poems, you will make progress on your own personal journey; that you will sink deeper into your own heart, as well as mine, and discover that space where the Spirit is caught and held.

Maureen McCarthy
May 1994

# *Acknowledgments*

Whenever a task such as this is undertaken it is not without conviction that many people will share the burden, willingly and gracefully. Because I have depended upon so many I wish to take this opportunity to express my thanks. The following friends who are mentioned are but a few who have shared in the adventure of this publication and deserve special recognition:

To Charles Rich, who urged the publication of these poems after reading them in 1993 and continued with encouragement and prayer to support the project.

To Norma Mosheim, who first collected the scraps and notes of the early poems and lovingly typed them.

To Donna Cavallaro, my secretary, for invaluable assistance with typing, mailings, and general organizing for the past year. She shares much of the credit and joy of seeing this work finally in print.

To Nancy Lane, for helping with the reading and correction of the manuscript.

To the community of St. Mary's Abbey, Wrentham, Mass., for hospitality, a place to rest, pray and listen.

To Miriam Pollard, OCSO, who insisted on the personalized illustrations, patiently supported the process, and has been both guide and mentor—pointing the way toward the garden and the goldfinch.

To Jennifer Durcan McCarthy, who assisted with suggestions on technique for the drawings.

To the monks of St. Joseph's Abbey, Spencer, Mass., who provided bounteous hospitality, nourishing the spiritual environment for Eugene and me.

To Bernard Bonowitz, OCSO, for presenting the opportunity to consider the imagery of these poems as pure gift.

To Gerald O'Collins, S.J. and Basil Pennington, OCSO, for praise and encouragement in all areas of the spirit, especially this little work.

To John and Esty Duff, for the gift of their hearts and Oakmarsh, the space and place to write during the annual August visit with my mother.

To my beloved husband, Eugene, for encouragement, love, understanding, pride and patience quite beyond my ability to describe.

# Songs of Joy

# Beginnings

Benevolent Father you have handed me
   A day, a year, a stretch of eternity,
The opportunity of prayer and work.
   Going forth, returning to myself and you;
A day of sunlight splashing on ferry planks.
   A glimpse of a shy, quiet man,
Newspaper all ready in hand,
   Clutched against the breezes from the water.

The summer begins, promising the best,
   A whole day to share and laugh
   With the sire of the line,
The man of contradictions,
   Dignity and grace.

To listen again to fabled tales,
   Finding truths, wisdom,
   And remembered power,
Laughing together as we
   Jubilantly accept the newest day.

## On the Beach

Dropping the nets
No time for good-byes,
Changing our lives
Forever.

"Follow me," He says.
 We mutely stumble along
 Behind him
 At last.

## The Promise

God the Father speaks,
"I love you my child,
More than you can understand,
More than you can possibly love yourself.
You are my creation,
My own special treasure."

"I will always hold you
In the deepest places of my heart,
And though you will try
To wander away someday,
I will never let you go."

## Arrival

All around me silence,
Layers of joy
Spindrifting aloneness,
Endlessly lapping sea and shore
Rocks sea and me to sleep.

## Homecoming

Perfect July night,
Golden amber meeting citron sky,
Dropping gently in the bay,
Tails limp,
Struggling to live,
Creeping to rest at anchor.
We wait it out together,
The old ship and me,
For tomorrow's promise
And another chance.

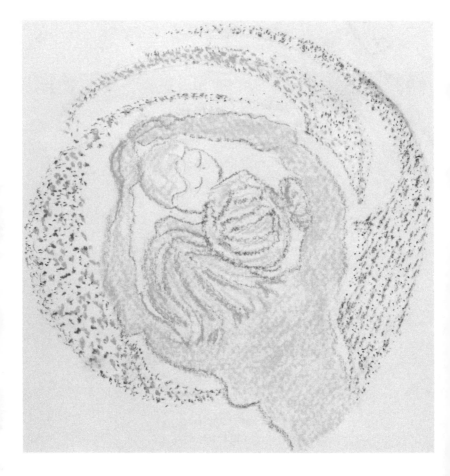

# *Woman*

To be woman is to know
Eternal truths,
Internally

It is to nourish and protect,
And understand,
Inevitably

To live a woman must create
When all is separate,
Totality

For her there is no mystery,
In giving self,
Continually

# *Visitors*

Perpetual day long,
Empty sounds and people,
Shadows dancing,
Calling, pleading.

No sense in the saying,
Nor in the crying.
The visit from restlessly
Anxiously young.
Garbled orders and then
They leave.

Someone comes to hold my hand,
Sometimes, so lovely;
But none sit quietly or stay.
I stay here and wonder
About the meaning of it all.

# Release

I am returning Lord
Take me home,
Not in my time, but yours.

Staying was not in my plan.
Going out with a band
I would have thought was
More my kind of style.
The Fourth of July might have been nice,
In keeping I think
With my charms.

O Lord for one more day
I will stay,
Watching uncertainly,
Listening desperately
For your call.

# Reminder

The statues watched,
The candles burned,
While all the pain poured out.

Tell me what to do.
Please, Lord, please.
I don't know what life's about.

What about the job, the kids,
School and parents and sex and me?
Where can I find myself?

The simple answer comes each time,
Insisting to be heard,
"Trust me, Trust me."

To trust you is so simple, Lord,
Is that why it is
So easy to forget?

# *Anniversary Reflections*

You tried to tell us long ago
That all was well with you
We could not let you go.
In our humanness we had to cling
To sorrow, needing it
To explore the cavities of pain.

In these days of understanding
We thank you for release,
From complexity, uncertainty,
From reasoning with suffering.
Now we try to thank you for the grace
Your pain has brought.

## Memorabilia

So we let them go
The symbols of our love,
The loosened teeth,
The scarred tissue,
The reminders of the pain.

Or do we recognize
That love is pain,
And pain is loving, never vainly?
Our vanity requires such tools
To remind us we can love.

## Farewells

Listen carefully to lichens growing on birches.
Watch intently as the last rose blooms.
Memorize the curl of wave, the reckless bird,
The chipmunks in their madcap race for food.
They all know nature's secret of
How to greet the winter.
But I will linger on the path a little longer
And vainly hope to stretch the autumn day.

# *Departure*

Into the nothingness
That is everything and everywhere
Into the void that fills
    My emptiness

More than entering
The arms of God
    Leaving me to BE
  Inside His very self

I am home,
I am ME.

# *Nostalgia*

Treading ancient paths,
Roaming the memorized streets,
Winds moaning, hearts mourning,
Where youth has taken the forceful turn.
Stopping off to stay with those
More wise than me
Who learned the tune
While I was busy trying to hear the music.

# *Eucharist*

Velvet comfort throbbing,
So rich, complete
Pushing, fighting, struggling
We thrust our life at life.

No refuge comes to greet us
No ultimate hand of safety
Timelessly suspended,
We often disconnect.

Until we finally locate
That other womb to bear us
The one we chose as if
The choice was ours.

We enter for return
The vital heat of Christ
The birth that is renewal
In the wound become a womb.

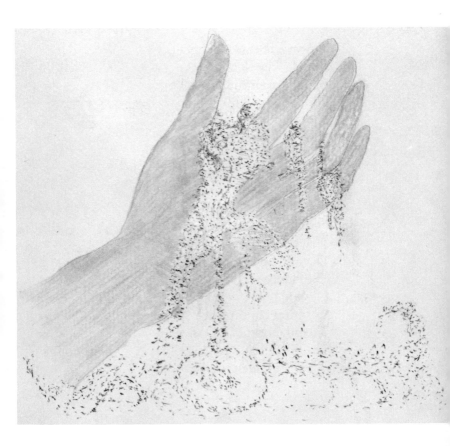

## Resurrection Song

Now my love, you hand me life,
Sharing beyond union,
Beyond growth into you.
In depth of senses,
Locating you,
In warmth, in water and in blood.

Drowning in the river
To lose myself and vanish
Inside you dissolving.

Into the bridegroom,
Exploding with joy.
The miracle happens,
New birth achieved,
Again and again in you
The birth of me.

# Songs for the Journey

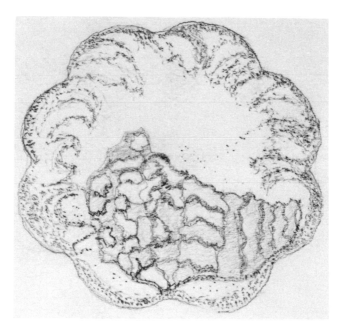

# Pilgrimage

Each year I walk the road with you,
    To try to memorize
The little things that made your journey
    So different from the rest.

Each time I take the steps
    In silent rhythm
I renew the mystery
    Of love and death and pain.

The years have mounted
    In measured pace
New meanings have been found in
    The love, the death, the loss.

Your image stays ahead in line
    I always lag behind.
The walking goes more smoothly
    In my giant's shadow.

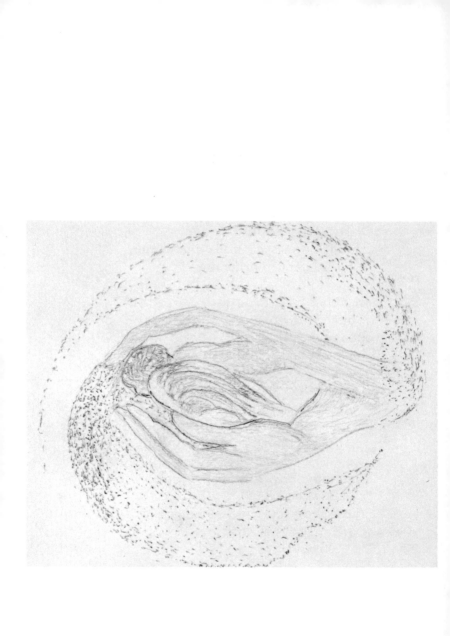

## Morning Song

Something about today buoyed the spirit,
And fueled the inner fires of love.
The clean morning air,
Sharply lingering night's acidity
Saffron shades of a newborn sun.

Soft light on metal growing stronger
Lifting, carrying us to realms
Temporarily detaching
From earthling mysteries,
Escaping from the genie's jar
To joust with clouds.

Not peace exactly,
But elements far flung.
In ancient origins of earth and sky
To wonder at creation's challenge
And learn the meaning of significance.

# Lauds

Beautiful day
Cold and clear,
Razor sharp sky
Flying strips of sunlight.

The park alive, beating,
Giant amoeba indecisively
Pulling in all directions.


# Mid-Day Prayer

I call constantly,
    Forgetting the calling,
Knowing that if I continue
    I will be heard,
    Answered.

Mary's ceaseless calling
    For a wandering child,
Joseph's ritual beckoning
    To duties,
    Work and prayer.

How much longer, louder
    Should I call,
Who cannot survive
    Without a response
Ensuring my reality.


## *None*


A high plateau beckons
    Softly I sit with limbs nestled.
Loosely arranged
    To repeat the chant.
        To wait,
        To listen,
While all the breath goes out
    And all of life comes surging
    In the very center of myself.

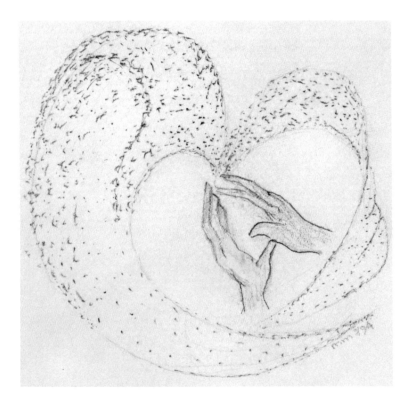

# Vespers

Here it is Lord,
  The ragged tatters of my day.
I lay it gently,
  Quietly at your feet
Knowing that my victories
  Have been few,
The defeats many.

My own arrogance
  Astounds me.
The closer I come to you
  The more this troubles me.
Now that I know its name
  I can hear it frequently.

In giving you all
  This burdensome day
All of it
  Becomes worthy.
This pitiful sacrifice
  Is suddenly magnificent
My "humbled heart" rejoices.

# Winter Song

Snow drifted down during the night
Lashing the branches together.
Outside my room a world is still,
Caught in motion, frozen.
Lonely lights describe life lived
Here on this planet until today.

All down the desolate caverns
The hollow howls echo
Lamenting a life of the past
Store windows flash back
In white icy sheets.
The isolate voyeur I search
For a record, a history
Of a life that vanished
With the moon last night.

Captive of the present moment,
Not yet the anticipated day,
I am the singular existing life force
Rejoicing in barren snowy hills.

## Escape

My mountain top is calling me
To come where none have been
To sit and wait for silent songs
Of beating wings that wish to fly.

My private space is cool and high,
Misty shrouds, dappled sun
Distant shadows, blue horizon
All noises fade and fall away.

The clanking beads, the rattled horns,
The garbled voices gossiping,
Muffled by a beating heart.

Higher and lighter
I am carried
To that wide plateau
Where I can sit in solitude
In extravagant spatial stretches,
Boundless emptiness.

The waiting comforts.
My senses are strong, central,
To exist, to be, is all.
For the rest it does not matter,
Not now, not ever,
Not on this mountain.

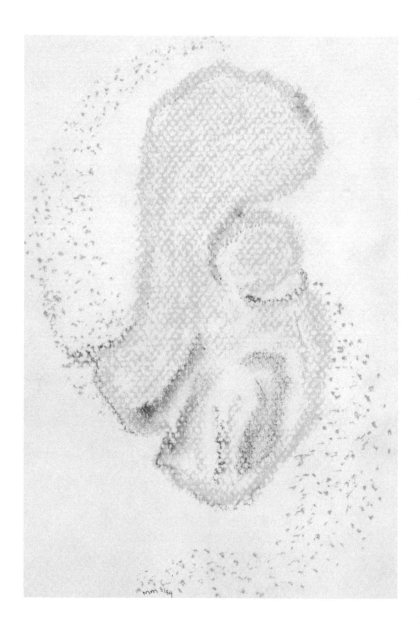

# *Nativity*

The merest child herself
She wondered once again
About the message
She had hidden in her heart
About the baby
She had hidden in her womb
About the million tiny miracles
Sleeping in her arms.

Young mother of the morning
Muses at the paradox
That this precious gift of life
Was grown in her body
Bathed in her blood.

Her eyes reflect his image
In the dawn of their first day
She whispers, as much to him
As to herself, so simply,
"This is my body
This is my blood."

# From A Maine Journal

Oh, God, I who am so unworthy
    Stand before you again.
I beg always for something,
    The greater like world peace,
The smaller like personal virtue.

In my humanness I often fail
    To understand the struggle
The continual need for suffering,
    For sacrifice, for pain.

Please help me to accept
    That each of us is  called uniquely
To suffer, to sacrifice ourselves.

Your own mother did not ask
    That your cross be lifted.
She to whom all favors would be granted
    Prayed instead for strength,
That you might do your Father's will
    And find victory in its accomplishment.

Grant that I may keep this always before me
    That I may support those for whom I care
With love, your love,
    With understanding, your understanding,
With patience to the end.

Help me to see your face again
    In the shadow of a cross.

# Chapel Windows

Each morning in bright succession
The magical spell is cast.
A majestic angel enters
Jade robes spilling on sunny fields.
Fiery wings lend power to the heralding
Arresting shepherds in frightened awe.

Below a queen holds court
With love displaying to stately visitors
A radiant, beaming Child.
Even wooden beams and manger bed
Seem regal in His light.

When evening comes the stable arch remains,
But moonlight floods the earthen floor,
Washes plaster walls and
Silhouettes the princely guests
Who stand the vigil
Til the angel sings again.

Following the pattern of the season
Each day the Child is born.
The angel chants the news again
And ancient kings keep watch.
While busy worlds flow by
The queen smiles wisely at
All of us who also kneel to pray
And contemplate her Son.

# Songs of the Goldfinch

# Vigils

Moon so full,
So bright.
Close enough to touch,
Brighter by far
Than stars are supposed to be.
Trees all black,
Against this light
Branches reach to crackled sky.
And stars!
Oh, the stars look out
Enough to make you gasp.

When all this
Midnight sorcery
Is hushed, stilled,
The earth's great heart
Stops throbbing.
In that silent moment
The goldfinch sings again.

# Courtship

In another space of time,
    A pause of life.
We walked a beach like this one,
Spilling out aimlessly
    Before the sea.
That silver shore confirmed a margin,
    Endless moments to foresee,
A future we could not know
    Or in the knowing understand.

You asked me if I would live with you
    Beside the sea some day.
Simplicity disguised concern,
    So simply did we arrange it.
Undreamed dimensions were explored
    That day and cast away
To urchins underfoot who were
    Shamelessly mute at the great gift.

This morning as I walk alone
    To greet dawn's crimson path,
The sea still claims the souvenirs
We cast so carelessly upon her shore.
Quite insistingly she asks,
    "What has become of you?"
In chant assuring me with every step.

Confidently I review the dialogue we've shared,
    Through the rising of the sun.
The task is clearer now as chill surrenders
    The grasp upon my bones,
Allowing me to search again for
    Remnants of the urchin shells.

Now I ask the day that has arrived with dawn,
    So breathlessly,
    Quite unexpectedly,
"Someday has come so soon,
    But where are we?"

# Yesterday

It was what we call Spring.
Their world was trembling with growing beauty.
In garden corners
Fertility burst forth.

He said, "I will hold you now and always.
In my heart is a place for you.
You will be mine I will be yours."
Forever was their kingdom.

A creeping called the sadness came
Into the garden spaces newly formed
In their hearts.
And pain came along too;
Now darkness replaced the light.

Darkness was a nuisance.
Sorrow and pain became a burden.
They sighed,
Struggled on.

The next Spring came bringing
Fertility in rapture.
It whispered of the possible.
At last the woman spoke.

Thoughtfully, articulately,
She gave consent
To a greater love than his
Or any other.

She flowered more gloriously
Than all that garden beauty,
Filled as she was
With his abundant seed.

# *Anniversary*

To share with each other again
The mysterious communication,
The loss of self in him,
    In her.
To know my strength lies in that loss.
At the very bottom
    Of the emptiness,
    Is the little key
To where my self has gone.
In giving up myself,
Growing in the depths of you,
    There is part of me.

More leisurely now, more comfortable,
    The tender gesture,
The glance across the space between.
In celebration or discouragement,
I find comfort in your strength,
Your trust confronts me with your hope,
    Defends me from myself,
And calming anxious fears destroys
    The limitations of my life.

We have come this far as one.
    We begin to glimpse the truth
About the emptiness of self.

I hear it in the commonplace of everyday,
    See it in your eyes,
Hold it sometimes in my hands.

In the journey which has brought us.
    To this place of constancy.
    I sense this last stability.
In this evening light we find a quiet,
    A reverence for the history
    That is our love.

# Reverie

Into our garden a woman walks today,
    Newly arrived,
    Breathlessly perfect,
Listening intently
To an imagined song.

A man sits in the shade talking to the children,
Telling them a fable
    Of a long forgotten time,
    His memory suddenly quite new.

The woman hugs the smallest ones,
    Drawing them to herself,
    Entering their hearts
With a remembered song
Of a moment in her life
    When time stood still.

The music sweetness echoes.
She has the melody in mind.
Her memory acknowledges the truth
She was given once to choose,
    Making a decision,
    Taking on a task,
That came to her in silence and alone.

From that quiet corner of her life
Came the Christmas Night
When all the world was taken in her arms,
    As the Wonderful Child,
    The Infant King
Became the purpose of her song.

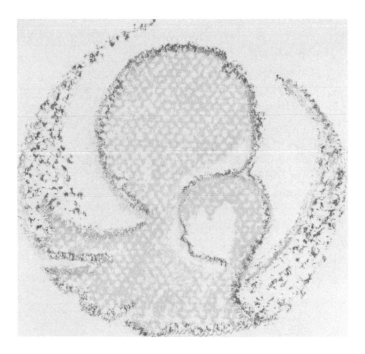

# *Solidarity*

Here we are in this place at last.
Busy Sabbath duties fall away behind us,
    All complete.
    Lovely stretch of hours,
Opening wide its arms,
Gathering us in.

The silent rain is falling everywhere,
    Around the cave,
    Upon the slab.
In the garden all is dim.

We are two school girls whispering together.
We are two old women sharing secret thoughts,
    Of life and death
    And all that lies between.

"Remember once when doors locked tight
    Flew open?
Remember all the lovely words we knew
    That turned the key?
The secret was to grab the word,
    To own it,
    Almost breathe it in."

"One day the word was 'mercy', wasn't it?
Remember how we picked it up,
    Looked inside, and
    Bravely tried it out.
You, of course, remember it,
    You showed me how."


"Suddenly a well locked door flew open.
A cross appeared spilling mercy at our feet,
    On the floor,
    All around us,
In all the space that was between."


"It was so long ago, or so I think,
    But now it's night.
You be *mercy* and I'll be *love*,
We'll wait together here.
    It isn't long at all to wait,
    When you're waiting for your son."

# Reflection

Sorrow lives in a stony place
At the very bottom of my garden.
      Not always, but often
      It seems to wake,
      Attempts to rise.

But it is there, it is always there,
It has been the companion of my days
      For so long, so very long,
      I do not call it by its name,
      But it is always there.

In activity it lies gently, very quietly.
Peace disturbs its rest.
      In the stillness of a dawn,
      Or after vespers in the dark,
      It calls to me and tries to be my friend.

I stay watchful most days
And especially at night.
      It takes a lot of vigilance
      To keep that stony place
      From living in my heart.

# Preparation Day

There will be Passover at my house,
 Although I am not ready.
My house cluttered, cramped
 Unready for a guest,
  This guest.

But ancient words unlock the doors,
 A struggling, fluttering thing
  That is my soul
Whispers counsels of confidence,
 "Accept, accept, accept."

The door swings wide
And love, the stranger,
 Stumbles in.

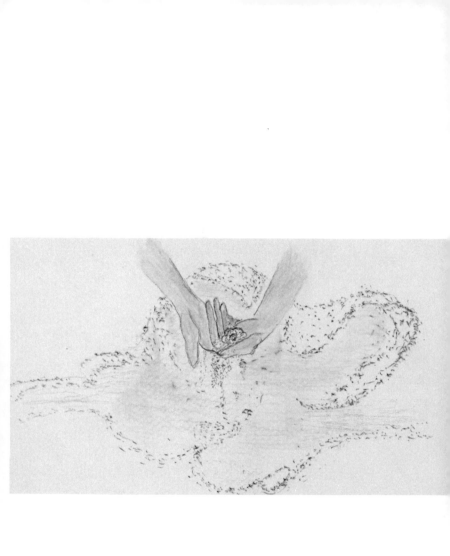

# Sea Shells

They were my treasures,
Gathered over many months
From all the seasons of my heart,
Recalling pieces of my history
Each shape so importantly a part.
Across the floor they lie abandoned,
Rows of silent faces unfurl my soul
    With woeful stares.

The moment comes to stand apart,
To push away each little face,
Not mine to hold or give away or
    Seek again at will.

No longer may I dream with them,
Or know the mystery of how they hide
    In secret places.
I begin to search the shore again
And see if memory can fit old friends
    With brand new faces.

# Singing in the Silence

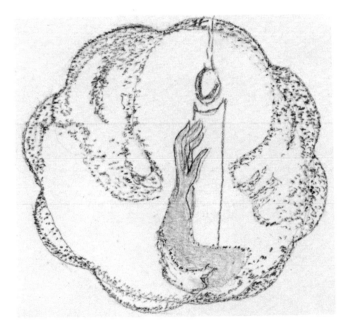

# The Gift

Again you have entered.
You have reached out
Strong arms have pulled me close.
You have reminded me.

You have allowed me to enter you
The pain is shared now.
The cold and empty spaces of my heart
Are wearing your love.

I am remembering
I am learning your sorrow
This bond is forever
I wind it back around your heart
Returning it to you.

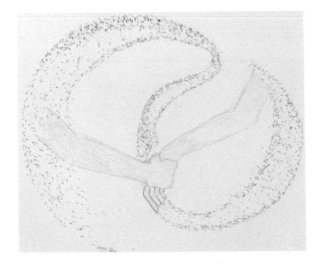

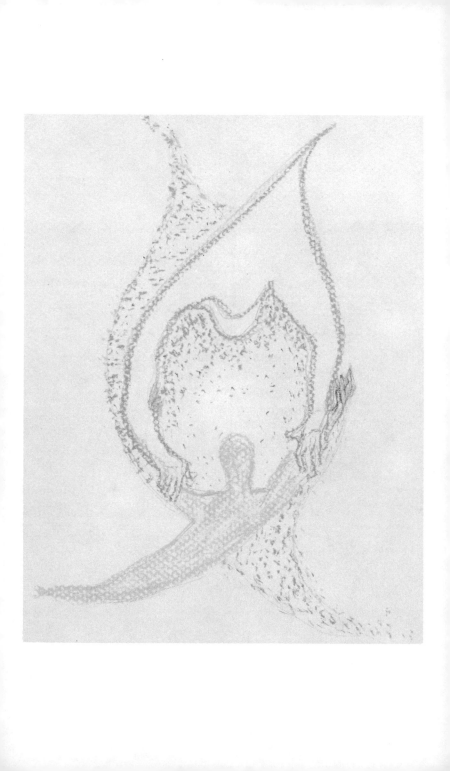

# The Meeting

Invade my body.
Ravish my soul
Reach to every cell,
      Every atom
Into every part of my being.

When I am complete,
A spirit saturated by love,
Allow me to carry your being.

To the world,
To each person I see
In each act I perform.

I am not only with you
You are not only with me,
I AM YOU.

## For Thomas

How many long years ago
Did I first hear those words,
Feel the horror,
The abandonment?

How many long years ago
Was I a child in sorrow,
Not understanding
The finality?

How many long years ago
Was I in pain,
Grieving the loss,
The escape?

## Coincidence

Seven years is a long short time,
An eternity in little stretches.
Do they understand?
Does it matter that they don't
Where there is no time except in the
Order of the hours.

# Meditation One

The ocean platter trembles,
    In sudden rush of rain.
Its gentle rhythm rocks,
    A constant monotone.

A soundless music chants,
    With syllables unstressed,
Changeless in its purpose
    The ceaseless tuneless hymn.

I hear the wordless patterns,
    In timeless meter sung.
Rising, falling, beating,
    The weary soul at prayer.

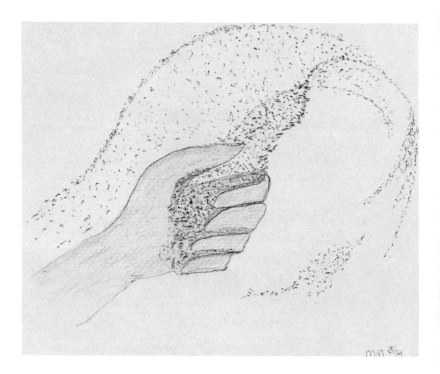

## In June

What can I **give**?

The space to grow,
The constancy of love,
The dignity of obedience.

What can I **do**?

Believe in all the dreams,
Explore all the realities,
Trust all the possibilities.

What can I **be**?

The helper, planner,
Mirror, lover, friend,
Eternally grateful wife.

## After Morning Prayer

Saturday in the endless day
November's sky broods,
Stares at us through bared branches
    As we walk
        He walks with us, surrounding us.

We catch frosted vapors on our tongues.
In the bleakness we rejoice
As we see him
    In one another,
        As we laughing mount the stair.

At breakfast we share in bread and conversation
And in our rituals and explanations
We discover that the King
Has come to visit
    Once again.

## In the Garden

How did the stars look
From Gethsemane?
Was there any consolation
For a suffering man?
      From the cold,
      From the stones,
      From the wind and air?

When his contemplation
Left him spent,
Did angels come to care?
Did they bathe and stroke him?
      With gentle hands,
      With soft voices,
      With patient strength?

# Evensong

Angels voices chant Magnificat
    By candlelight.
The order of each day
    Fixed and firm
    In prayer and work.

Harmony of life uninterrupted
    In silent rhythm.
Each day is changeless
    Predictable
    Incessant
As waves upon shores drumming
    Relentless tunes.

Nocturnal chants of angels
    Praising Mary
No longer send me lifting
    Dreaming
Now mine the prayers fixing
    Life's reality.

## Lady of Sorrow

Tonight I walk with you,
Let me come,
Through the Passion and the Cross.

Each small sigh
Becomes a mantra,
Song for a broken heart.

I see in the crowds,
Watching the shame,
The disgrace, the brutality.

But as you approach
There is that look;
Majesty in your pain.

And what do I hear?
You are praying for us,
Forgiving the cruelty.

And you continue to pray.
Even now I can hear you
As you watch a dying son.

# Night Prayer

The day is finishing, dearest Jesus,
My duties come to an end.
Each day my love for you grows stronger,
And the days grow more rewarding.

I hear my own arrogance now,
Where before there were no voices.
I see my lack of charity
Pervasive and insistent.

I understand in little ways
That it is to you I have been so proud.
I have withheld myself from you
Who never knew the meaning of the word.

Forgive me once again
As I strive to mend my ways.
Tomorrow I will try harder
To keep you in every moment.

It is in keeping you with me
That I lose the arrogance of self,
And I find the charity of spirit
With which to start another day.